Marvell

Poems chosen by
Richard Brown and Kate Ruttle

Illustrated by David Parkins

CAMBRIDGE
UNIVERSITY PRESS

Cambridge Reading

General Editors
Richard Brown and Kate Ruttle

Consultant Editor
Jean Glasberg

PUBLISHED BY THE PRESS SYNDICATE OF THE UNIVERSITY OF CAMBRIDGE
The Pitt Building, Trumpington Street, Cambridge CB2 1RP

CAMBRIDGE UNIVERSITY PRESS
The Edinburgh Building, Cambridge CB2 2RU, United Kingdom
40 West 20th Street, New York, NY 10011-4211, USA
10 Stamford Road, Oakleigh, Melbourne 3166, Australia

Marvel Paws
This selection © Richard Brown and Kate Ruttle 1996
Illustrations © David Parkins 1996

This book is in copyright. Subject to statutory exception and to the provisions of relevant collective licensing agreements, no reproduction of any part may take place without written permission.

First published 1996
Reprinted 1998

Typeset in Concorde

Printed in the United Kingdom at the University Press, Cambridge

A catalogue record for this book is available from the British Library

ISBN 0 521 49996 8 paperback

Acknowledgements

We are grateful to the following for permission to reproduce poems:
'Jemima Jane' by Marchette Chute from *Around and About* by Marchette Chute. Copyright 1957 by E.P. Dutton. Copyright renewed 1984 by Marchete Chute. Reprinted by permission of Elizabeth M. Roach.
'Cats' by Eleanor Farjeon from *Seeing and Doing*. Published by Thames TV, 1977.
'Mice' by Rose Fyleman. Reprinted by permission of The Society of Authors as the literary representative of the Estate of Rose Fyleman.
'I Want . . .' © Wes Magee, 1995.
'Marvel Paws' © Tony Mitton, 1996.
'Granny Goat' by Brian Moses. First Published in *Twinkle Twinkle Chocolate Bar* ed. John Foster. Oxford University Press.
'My Parakeet' by Grace Nichols. Copyright © Grace Nichols, 1991. Reproduced with permission of Curtis Brown Group Ltd, London on behalf of Grace Nichols.
'A Wriggly Riddle' © Joan Poulson, 1996.
'My Dog Spot' © Rodney Bennett.

Every effort has been made to reach copyright holders; the publishers would like to hear from anyone whose rights they have unknowingly infringed.

Contents

Marvel Paws *Tony Mitton* 4

A Wriggly Riddle *Joan Poulson* 7

My Parakeet *Grace Nichols* 9

My Dog, Spot *Rodney Bennett* 10

Cats *Eleanor Farjeon* 13

Jemima Jane *Marchette Chute* 14

Mice *Rose Fyleman* 17

My Puppy *Aileen Fisher* 18

Granny Goat *Brian Moses* 20

I Want . . . *Wes Magee* 22

Index of first lines 24

Marvel Paws

Marvel Paws
is a magic cat.
She dreams up spells
on the kitchen mat.
She walks the length
of the garden wall.
Then POP!
she isn't there
at all . . .

Marvel Paws
is a flicker of fur,
a rustle of grass
and a quiet purr.
Marvel Paws
is an empty dish,
an upset jug
and a missing fish.

Marvel Paws
is a magic cat.
She has no cloak
or magic hat.
But I know by the way
her whiskers twitch
that Marvel Paws
is a pussycat witch.

Tony Mitton

A Wriggly Riddle

My pet is
wriggly and wiggly
I don't lock him away

I lie in the garden
to talk to him
I see him every day

he's smooth and round
he's pinky-brown
he's the best
pet in the world

my wriggly-wiggly
smooth and squirmy
pinky-browny worm.

Joan Poulson

My Parakeet

Anyone see my parakeet, Skeet?
He's small and neat,
He's really sweet,
With his pick-pick beak,
And his turn-back feet.

Skeet, Skeet, I wouldn't tell a lie
You are the green-pearl of my eye.

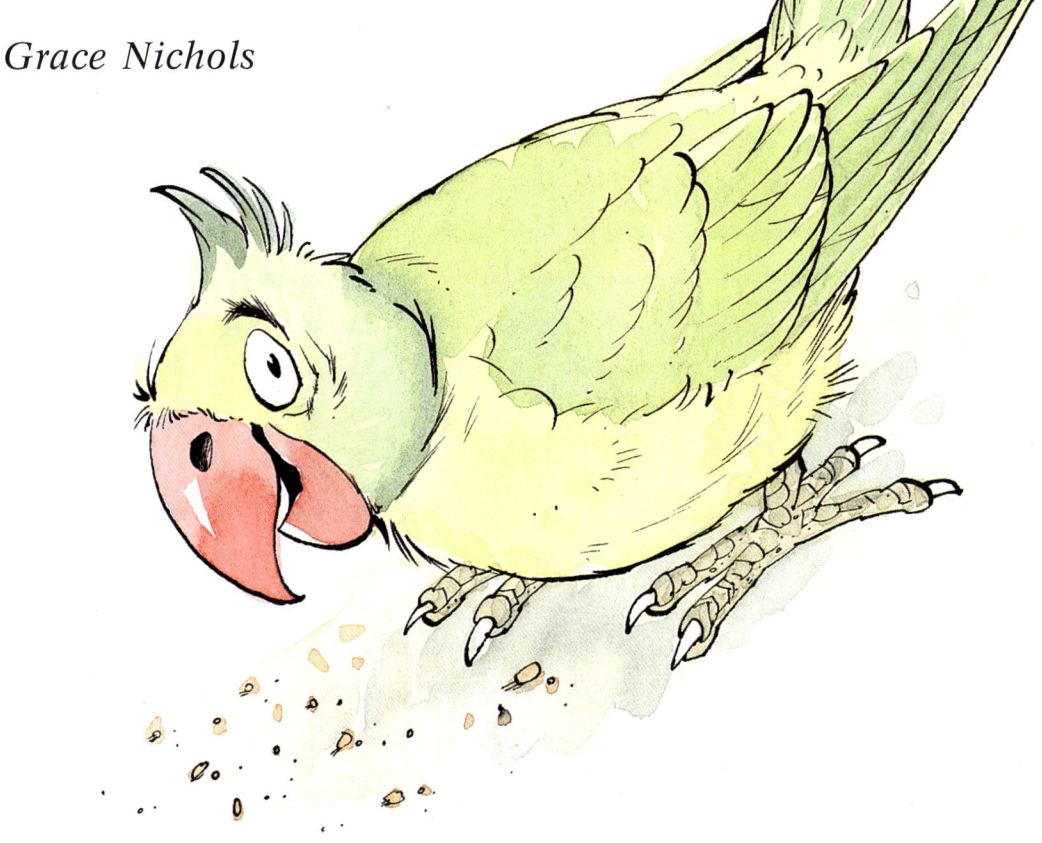

Grace Nichols

My Dog, Spot

I have a white dog
   Whose name is Spot,
And he's sometimes white
   And he's sometimes not.
But whether he's white
   Or whether he's not,
There's a patch on his ear
   That makes him Spot.

He has a tongue
  That is long and pink,
And he lolls it out
  When he wants to think,
He seems to think most
  When the weather is hot.
He's a wise sort of dog,
  Is my dog, Spot.

He likes a bone
   And he likes a ball,
But he doesn't care
   For a cat at all.
He waggles his tail
   And he knows what's what,
So I'm glad that he's my dog,
   My dog, Spot.

Rodney Bennett

Cats

Cats sleep
Anywhere,
Any table,
Any chair,
Top of piano,
Window-ledge,
In the middle,
On the edge,
Open drawer,
Empty shoe,
Anybody's
Lap will do,
Fitted in a
Cardboard box,
In the cupboard
With your frocks –
Anywhere!
They don't care!
Cats sleep
Anywhere.

Eleanor Farjeon

Jemima Jane

Jemima Jane,
   Oh, Jemima Jane,
She loved to go out
   And slosh in the rain.
She loved to go out
   And get herself wet,
And she had a duck
   For her favourite pet.

Every day
  At half-past four
They'd both run out
  The kitchen door;
They'd find a puddle,
  And there they'd stay
Until it was time
  To go away.

They got quite wet,
   But they didn't mind;
And every rainy
   Day they'd find
A new way to splash
   Or a new way to swim.
And the duck loved Jane,
   And Jane loved him.

Marchette Chute

Mice

I think mice
Are rather nice.

Their tails are long,
Their faces small,
They haven't any
Chins at all.
Their ears are pink,
Their teeth are white,
They run about
The house at night.
They nibble things
They shouldn't touch
And no one seems
To like them much.

But *I* think mice
Are nice.

Rose Fyleman

My Puppy

It's funny
my puppy
knows just how I feel.

When I'm happy
he's yappy
and squirms like an eel.

When I'm grumpy
 he's slumpy
and stays at my heel.

It's funny
 my puppy
knows such a great deal.

Aileen Fisher

Granny Goat

Eat anything
will granny goat,
handkerchiefs,
the sleeve of your coat,
sandwiches,
a ten pound note,
eat anything
will granny goat.

Granny goat
goes anywhere,
into the house
if you're not there,
follows you round,
doesn't care,
granny goat
goes anywhere.

Granny goat
will not stay
tied up
throughout the day,
chews the rope,
wants to play,
granny goat
won't stay

anywhere you
want her to,
she would rather be
with YOU!

Brian Moses

I Want . . .

Richard owns a rabbit
Chloe's got a cat
Tricia has a terrapin
But me?
I want a *rat*!

Barry loves his budgie
Donna walks her dog
Parma rides his pony
But me?
I want a *frog*!

Harry holds his hamster
Pauline's pigeons coo
Gerry feeds his gerbil
But me?
I want a *zoo*!

Wes Magee

Index of first lines

Anyone see my parakeet, Skeet?   9

Cats sleep   13

Eat anything   20

I have a white dog   10

I think mice   17

It's funny   18

Jemima Jane   14

Marvel Paws   4

My pet is   7

Richard owns a rabbit   22